HSV MP2   5322
Chocolate

SIGHTSEERS
ESSENTIAL TRAVEL GUIDES TO THE PAST

AZTECS
& INCAS

A GUIDE TO TWO GREAT
EMPIRES IN 1504

Sue Nicholson

KING*fisher*

KINGFISHER
Kingfisher Publications Plc
New Penderel House,
283–288 High Holborn,
London WC1V 7HZ

Editor   Camilla Reid
Senior Designer   Jane Tassie

Illustrations   Inklink Firenze
Kevin Maddison

Additional design   Veneta Altham
Cormac Jordan
DTP Co-ordinator   Nicky Studdart
Production Controllers   Jacquie Horner
Caroline Jackson
Picture Research Manager   Jane Lambert
Proofreader   Emma Wild
Indexer   Hilary Bird

First published by Kingfisher Publications Plc 2000
1 3 5 7 9 10 8 6 4 2

1TR/0500/WKT/ATLS/140MA

A CIP catalogue record for this book is available from
the British Library.

ISBN 0 7534 0412 5

Printed in
Hong Kong/China

Contents

Introducing Mexico

Visitors to Aztec lands will be rewarded by a truly memorable experience. Although the climate can be harsh, the scenery is stunning and there is plenty to see and do. Most Aztecs live in or near the capital city of Tenochtitlan, built on an island in Lake Texcoco in the central Valley of Mexico. It will make an ideal base for your holiday.

The central valley is surrounded by high snow-capped peaks. To the southeast, see if you can make out the active volcano Popocatepetl, whose name means 'Smoking Mountain'.

Look out for drawings or carvings of an eagle sitting on a prickly pear cactus, eating a snake. According to legend, this was a sign sent by the god Huitzilopochtli around 175 years ago. It told the Aztecs to settle on the swampy island in Lake Texcoco.

In just under two centuries, Tenochtitlan has grown into a huge, complex city and is now home to around 200,000 people. It is divided into four districts – the Place of the Gods (the temple compound), the Heron's Home, Flowery Meadow and Mosquito Fen, where the local people live and work.

Moctezuma has been the Aztec ruler for two years and is extremely popular with the locals.

To the north of the Valley of Mexico lie dusty deserts. To the south, there are tropical rainforests.

In the Aztec language, Tenochtitlan means 'place of the fruit of the cactus'.

Tenochtitlan is linked to the land by causeways. An aqueduct running parallel to the western causeway brings fresh water to the city from the mountains.

Sightseers' tip The best time to catch the stunning views of the surrounding mountains and volcanoes is at dawn, before the city is enveloped in a cloud of smoke produced by thousands of cooking fires.

The emperor, or tlatoani, Moctezuma Xocoyotzin lives in the palace at the heart of the city. Parts of the palace were burned in a fire four years ago, so are currently closed for rebuilding works.

Getting around

Tenochtitlan is made up of an intricate network of canals and waterways, so hiring a canoe to get around is a must. People use boats for everything, whether they are shopping, fishing or just visiting friends and family. Boats vary in size, from a one-person hollowed-out canoe to a larger vessel that takes five people in comfort.

Sightseers' tip The main canals are bordered by earth pavements, so it is possible to travel by foot in some places. Why not take a leisurely stroll along one of the broad avenues that lead to Moctezuma's palace?

If you can afford it, hire a litter to carry you in style. However, this mode of transport is usually reserved for the tlatoani himself, so be prepared to talk yourself out of trouble if questioned.

As you paddle around the edges of the city, look out for the chinampas, or cultivated gardens. This reclaimed land is shored up by willow twigs and branches and is used to grow fruit, flowers and vegetables. Space in Tenochtitlan is at a premium, so only married couples have the right to live on and farm the chinampas.

Be prepared for lots of walking – the Aztecs do not use wheeled vehicles.

Always keep on the right side of the law. Crimes are punished severely.

Don't expect a nightlife. Ordinary Aztecs believe spirits will steal their souls, if they stay out after dark.

If you are planning a long journey, you could join a trading trip organised by the pochteca, the powerful society of merchants. Unless you're fit enough to carry your luggage, you'll need to employ a porter. And, be warned, the merchants are so secretive about their business that they make all their excursions under the cover of darkness.

Out and about and desperate for the toilet? Don't worry. Keep an eye out for wicker cabins on city streets or country roads. Human waste is collected from these public lavatories, loaded onto big barges, then transported to the chinampas to be used as fertilizer.

7

What to wear

In summer, daytime temperatures can soar to 35°C, so it is best to adopt local dress to keep cool. Men and boys should wear a white loincloth, with the option of a plain cloak knotted over one shoulder. Women and girls wear loose tunics over long skirts. Most people go barefoot although warriors, and sometimes nobles, wear sandals.

Ordinary people's clothes are made out of coarse cloth, woven from the maguey cactus. The clothes of the nobility are made of fine cotton, and may be edged with fur, or embroidered around the hem.

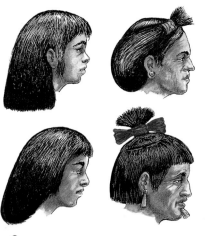

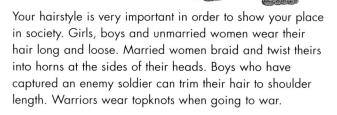

Your hairstyle is very important in order to show your place in society. Girls, boys and unmarried women wear their hair long and loose. Married women braid and twist theirs into horns at the sides of their heads. Boys who have captured an enemy soldier can trim their hair to shoulder length. Warriors wear topknots when going to war.

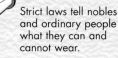 Red cochineal dye for cloth is made from the bodies of tiny crushed insects.

Strict laws tell nobles and ordinary people what they can and cannot wear.

 People believe that wearing jewellery will protect them from harm.

Moctezuma has declared a mini-war with the neighbouring state of Tlaxcala, and at any time you may hear the war drums summoning all males over the age of 15 to battle. Look out for the elite jaguar or eagle knights dressed from head to toe in jaguar skins or feathers. Weapons include axes and clubs called maquahuitl, which are spiked with sharp splinters of glassy obsidian rock.

Brooches and necklaces made of pearls and turquoise are popular, as are lip-plugs, nose-plugs and earrings. Only nobles are permitted to wear gold jewellery.

Sightseers' tip If you see a woman wearing make-up then it is probably her wedding day. Brides use yellow facepaint and red dye on their lips and teeth.

Food and drink

Most people drink water, but on special occasions pulque, a beer made from the sap of the maguey cactus, is often served. It's best to refuse this potent brew as only the elderly are permitted to touch it.

If the hunting has been good, you may be offered goose, pelican or fresh fish caught from the lake.

If you enjoy spicy food, then you're in for a culinary treat. Try dishes flavoured with hot chillis or, if you can't take the heat, those containing milder sweet peppers or honey. Local staples include tortillas (crisp pancakes), tamales (steamed dumplings), atole (a kind of maize, or sweetcorn, porridge), beans and vegetable stew.

Don't get too friendly with an Aztec family's dog – you may find it served for supper! These small, hairless hounds are kept as family pets, fattened up and eventually eaten.

If you are invited to a noble's house for the evening, you can usually expect turkey, duck and venison. You may also be offered an expensive frothy chocolate drink made from cocoa beans and sweetened with honey and vanilla.

Sightseers' tip Don't drink water from the lake! It has been seriously polluted by the manufacture of whitewash, a thin paint used on houses to reflect the sun's rays, and help keep the rooms inside cool.

Try the local delicacy – green slime skimmed from Lake Texcoco. It tastes a bit like cheese!

Don't expect to use knives, forks or spoons – people eat with their fingers.

Wondering why chocolate is so pricey? Cocoa beans are also used as money.

If you stay with a local family, you may be asked to lend a hand grinding maize on the stone metlatl. The flour is then shaped into tortillas and fried on a griddle, called a comal.

Accommodation

Staying with a local family is the best option in busy, central Tenochtitlan, but expect to share a room. Most town houses are built around a courtyard, and are home to up to 15 people. In the ordinary thatched cottages on the chinampas, the whole family will live in just one or two rooms.

Every household uses three-legged terracotta bowls to store drinking water or food. In smart homes, these are beautifully decorated.

You'll find top of the range accommodation in the home of a noble family. This type of house has three or four bedrooms, two spacious reception rooms (one for men and one for women) and a kitchen. Meals are served in the dining room, and you'll have servants to wait on you.

Sightseers' tip
Don't worry if you forget to pack your alarm clock. The whole of Tenochtitlan is woken at sunrise by local priests blowing trumpets made from giant conch shells – so there's no danger of oversleeping!

Don't expect a soft, comfy bed. Most people sleep on a reed mat rolled out on the floor.

You should expect just two meals a day – one a few hours after sunrise, the other in the evening.

Food is rationed to one tortilla for children from 3 to 5 years, rising to two for those over 13.

All houses contain a small shrine for the family to worship the gods. Many ordinary people honour the maize goddess, Xilonen.

The houses of the nobility may have one or two storeys. Their shaded balconies, cool fountains and lush gardens make them the ideal place to escape the heat of the midday sun.

After a day's sightseeing, why not take a refreshing steam bath? The mudbrick room is heated by a fire outside. You make the steam by throwing water on the walls inside.

Shopping

No visit to Tenochtitlan is complete without a trip to the market. It is incredibly busy, with up to 60,000 traders and visitors each day. Don't worry though, even though it's bustling, it's well organized and divided into areas according to what's on sale, so it's easy to find your way round.

Sightseers' tip If you think you're being cheated or you need help in some way, make for the long, open-sided hall in the middle of the market. Officials there will settle any disputes.

14

The noise from the market can be heard five kilometres away.

 Most goods are bartered, but cocoa beans or quills filled with gold dust are also used as money.

Look out for doctors tending their patients at the market. Herbs are sold as remedies.

One of the most fragrant parts of the market is that devoted to flowers. Also look out for heaps of spices and the brilliantly-coloured feathers used to edge robes or make headdresses.

Whatever souvenirs you want to buy, you'll find them at the market! Look out for cheap, locally-made sandals, woven cloth, baskets and ceramics. Goods brought in from further afield, such as shells from the coast, jade or turquoise, are more pricey. If you're tired of shopping and bartering, you can stop for a snack, have your hair cut, or get your fortune told.

If you're interested in a craft, such as featherworking or ceramics, why not visit the craftspeople at work? They belong to guilds and work in different areas of the city. Ask a local for directions.

Avoid getting mixed up in the part of the market where slaves are sold. Some slaves are prisoners who have been captured in war. Others may be Aztec people who have committed a crime and lost their freedom.

15

Sports and leisure

If you're a sports enthusiast, make sure you take in a game of tlachtli during your visit. It is fast-paced and tough – and very popular with the spectators. Not only is it exciting to watch, but tlachtli has religious significance too, standing for the battle between darkness and light. The ball symbolizes the Moon and the Sun, and the court represents the world.

On most street corners, you can see locals playing the gambling game of patolli. Players move coloured counters across the board according to the throw of marked, numbered beans.

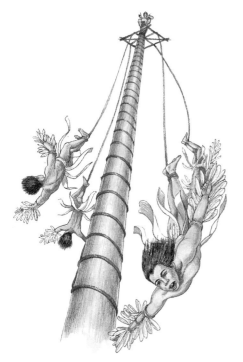

Depending on what time of year you visit, you may be able to see the flying festival in which four men dressed as birds leap from a high pole to honour the gods.

In tlachtli, it is forbidden for hands or feet to touch the solid rubber ball – only hips and knees can be used. The battle between the two teams to score the most hoops is long and hard. Some of the players may have bet all their possessions on the game.

Hundreds of people take part in dances held on important feast days.

After school, children must attend religious school to learn music and dance.

In tlachtli, the losing team may sometimes be sacrificed to the gods.

Be prepared to lose your cloak, if you go to a ball game. Winning teams may be entitled to take the spectators' clothes and belongings!

If sport isn't your thing, you could go to a concert or take part in a feast-day dance. Aztec musical instruments include flutes, bells and rattles. This teponaztli, or two-toned wooden drum, has a decorative owl carving on its side.

The palace

The royal palace has up to 500 visitors each day, who come to present tribute (a form of tax) to the tlatoani. Only rulers and nobles are allowed into the palace, but if you are lucky you may be invited as a guest. Don't expect to see Moctezuma himself though, even if you're in the same room. It is forbidden to look directly at him.

The day-to-day running of the empire is carried out by the tlatoani's deputy, Cihuacoatl, and hundreds of other officials.

Scribes keep the palace records in folding books called codices. Instead of writing, they use picture symbols, known as glyphs. All tribute goods presented to the emperor, such as jade necklaces, honey, headdresses or blankets, are documented.

The palace is huge and there is too much to see in a single day. It has thousands of rooms, including dining halls, libraries and lawcourts, and even a secret treasure house. There are also separate apartments for women, for the ruler's many wives, and for his 3,000 servants.

Sightseers' tip

Try to fit in a tour of the palace's magnificent gardens and zoo. The zoo contains many exotic and rare creatures, including quetzal birds, whose long, brilliantly-coloured plumes are prized by featherworkers.

All the neighbouring towns and cities conquered by the Aztecs must send tribute to the emperor. If they fail to do so, they face attack by his powerful army.

19

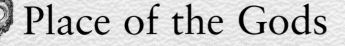

Place of the Gods

If you are feeling brave, visit the main temple complex in the heart of Tenochtitlan. Dominated by the Great Temple pyramid, it consists of several temples, as well as the priests' living quarters. However, make sure you avoid being in the complex when the Aztecs make their sacrifices to the gods.

Sightseers' tip

Don't faint if you see Aztecs pricking their fingers with the spine of a cactus to draw blood. People leave the spines in their local temple as offerings to the Sun god.

The Aztecs believe that human sacrifice keeps their gods happy, and so prevents the world from ending. During times of sacrifice, the steps of the Great Temple are drenched in the blood of the victims killed on altars at the top.

Look out for one of the thousands of priests that live in the temple complex. They are easy to spot as they blacken their faces with soot and do not cut their hair. You may well want to give them a wide berth as they are the people who perform the sacrifices.

Look out for the gruesome rack of skulls which stands in the complex.

The Aztecs need to be at war constantly in order to supply the priests with prisoners for sacrifice.

 The Great Temple has been enlarged many times. It is now 30 metres tall.

Steep steps at the front of the Great Temple lead to twin shrines at the top, dedicated to Tlaloc, the god of rain and fertility, and Huitzilopochtli, the god of the Sun and war. Each shrine houses a huge gold statue of the god, and the walls are richly decorated with carvings and paintings.

The Aztec people celebrate small local fiestas throughout the year. Try to attend a ceremony to celebrate the birth of a baby. It will be a joyful occasion with plenty of music and dancing.

Don't miss seeing the Stone of the Sun. This calendar measures the Aztec year, which is 360 days long, with five unlucky days at the end. At the centre is the face of the Sun god.

21

Trip into the mountains

For a change of scene, take a trip south to the empire of the Inca people. Be prepared to ford rivers and hack through tropical forests. Once you reach Inca lands, however, getting around is easy due to the well-maintained roads. The Incas' network of highways covers all 800,000 square kilometres of this vast empire, even allowing easy access to the high Andes mountains.

If you run short of supplies on the road, look out for a storehouse. These buildings are run by the government, and hold food and clothing for people in times of need.

If you need to send a message, enlist the help of a quipocamayo, someone trained in making and reading quipus. These knotted bundles of coloured string can record all sorts of information. A runner will carry it anywhere in the empire.

Although Incas are very hardy, even they find it chilly in the mountains. You will need a poncho made from llama wool, and a knitted cap.

Sightseers' tip

It's advisable to hire a llama to carry your bags on the steep mountain roads. Don't drive it too hard though, or it will sit down, refuse to move and spit!

The present Inca ruler is Huayna Capac, known as Sapa Inca.

 Avoid travelling in spring because of flash floods in the mountains.

Ordinary people are often made to work on building projects all over the empire.

Be ready to pay a toll to cross one of the many suspension bridges that you will encounter. Although they may be shaky, they are cleverly constructed and quite safe!

The golden city

During the great festival in December, hundreds of gold and silver objects are buried as sacrifices to the Sun god.

At the heart of the Inca empire lies Cuzco, the administrative and religious capital. If you plan to stay in the city, make sure to dress in the finest clothes and wear plenty of gold and silver jewellery, because only rich and important people live here. Your first stop in Cuzco should be the magnificent Temple of the Sun. With its gold-plated walls and a huge image of Inti, the Sun god, at its centre, it makes an awesome sight.

Take a walk to the area of Cuzco where the master goldsmiths live, and you can watch precious metals being worked into jewellery and ornaments. First the metal is melted, then it is poured into moulds. Finally, with great skill, it is beaten and soldered into shape.

Sightseers' tip Don't forget that Cuzco is in an earthquake zone. If a building starts to shake, stand under the door lintel and don't panic – Inca houses are built to survive even severe tremors. The stones may move, but they won't collapse.

Alongside the Sun Temple is the Golden Garden. This stunning attraction contains life-sized models of animals and plants, all made from pure gold. You might even spot the Sapa Inca and his wives there.

Incas call gold 'sweat of the Sun' and silver 'tears of the Moon'.

The streets of Cuzco are laid out in the shape of a puma, a sacred Inca animal.

Listen out for the delicate notes made by the panpipes, a popular Inca musical instrument.

The Incas are expert builders. Temples, forts and houses are made from large stone blocks, each shaped to fit together perfectly. Workers pull the blocks up ramps on wooden rollers, then lever them into place with long poles.

Outpost of the empire

Venture north from Cuzco into the Andes and you'll reach Machu Picchu, a spectacular fortress city carved into the side of a mountain. The best way to experience life in this isolated outpost is to stay with a local farming family in their stone cottage. The accommodation will be basic though, as most homes have just one room, shared by the whole family.

Don't trip over a guinea pig when you step inside an Inca home. They are fattened up on scraps, then end up in the pot themselves.

Inca women work hard, all day long. When not labouring in the fields, they must weave all their family's cloth on a backstrap loom.

Sightseers' tip Every family must give a proportion of the cloth and food they produce to the government as a kind of tax.

You may get fed up with potatoes by the end of your trip. Mountain people eat them at nearly every meal.

Everyone in Machu Picchu gets up early to tend their maize, quinoa (a type of grain) and other crops. Each family must work on their ruler's fields as well as their own. They also assist their neighbours when a crop needs planting or harvesting. As only the sons of nobles go to school, most children spend the day helping their parents – gathering herbs, herding llamas or carrying firewood.

Ordinary people have little furniture, so be prepared to sleep on the floor.	Important religious festivals are held at the beginning of each growing season.	Inca nobles are wealthy and live in well-built houses with plenty of servants.

Terraces are cut into the hillside to make level fields for the crops.

As a rule, most Inca people are law-abiding and hardworking. Every household shares a leader with 10–15 other families. The leaders report to local rulers, who report to provincial governors. They, in turn, report to one of four governors who answer to the Sapa Inca himself.

Survival guide

To keep things running smoothly and to closely control their large empires, both Aztec and Inca societies are highly-organized and strict. There is a great deal of bureaucracy, and you will need permission to travel anywhere. But although life is often tough for ordinary citizens, you will notice that few people are hungry or homeless.

Law and order

Laws are harsh and law-breakers are severely punished. The penalty for many crimes is death. In Aztec society, first offenders may lose their home. If they commit the same crime again, they are killed.

Badly behaved Aztec children are sometimes held over a fire containing chilli peppers. This harsh punishment hurts their throats and makes their eyes stream.

Health

Both Aztec and Inca doctors use a mixture of herbal medicine and common sense to heal the sick. If you fall ill, though, be careful. Some herbal drugs are quite dangerous and kill rather than cure. Inca doctors also rely on prayers and charms to cure patients, and often conduct healing rituals in the cold mountain rivers.

Before you travel, consult an Aztec priest to see whether the day is lucky or unlucky.

Inca men always carry with them a small bag containing a lucky charm.

If a member of a calpulli breaks the law, the whole calpulli may be punished.

The coca plant is more highly valued by the Incas than gold and silver. They believe it has sacred powers and often burn it in temples. The leaves are also chewed to give a person energy or to overcome nausea.

Administration

Aztec towns and cities are divided into calpullis, or clans. Tenochtitlan alone has about 80 calpullis. Each calpulli is responsible for its own part of the city. It has its own temple and school, and makes sure the streets are swept every day and the sewage removed. It also cares for the sick and elderly.

Even though they have many laws, the Aztecs believe it is their gods who ultimately rule their lives. They try to positively influence the gods by giving gifts and offering them sacrifices.

❓ Souvenir quiz

Your trip to the Aztec lands in the Valley of Mexico and the Inca empire in the Andes is over. Try this souvenir quiz to see how much you can remember from your visit. You will find the answers on page 32.

1. What does the name of the Aztec's main city, Tenochtitlan, mean in the Aztec language?

a) Eagle eating a snake.

b) The lands beside the water.

c) Place of the prickly pear cactus.

2. Why should you not get too friendly with an Aztec family's dog?

a) It may be sacrificed at the top of the Great Temple in the centre of Tenochtitlan.

b) You may be upset if it ends up in the family's stewing pot and is served for supper.

c) You may be made to breathe smoke from a fire containing chilli peppers as a punishment.

3. How do you take a bath, Aztec-style?

a) You sit in one of the wicker cabins lining the city streets and roads.

b) You jump off a chinampa into Lake Texcoco and scrub yourself all over with green slime and maize flour.

c) You sit inside a mudbrick room while someone stokes the fire outside. Water poured on the walls makes the steam rise.

4. Which goods on sale at the market are probably the most expensive?

a) Locally made sandals and woven cloth.

b) Food grown on the chinampas, such as maize, tomatoes and peppers.

c) Shells and semi-precious stones.

5. What does the Aztec word tlachtli describe?

a) A flying festival in which four men leap from a high pole to honour the gods.

b) A fast-paced ball game in which two teams try to knock a ball through a stone ring.

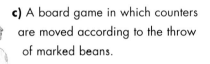

c) A board game in which counters are moved according to the throw of marked beans.

6. How do Aztec girls wear their hair?

a) Trimmed to their shoulders then tied in a topknot.

b) Long and loose.

c) Plaited then twisted into horns at the sides of their heads.

7. What is an Aztec calpulli responsible for?

a) Keeping order and settling disputes at the market.

b) Looking after a particular district or part of a city.

c) Sacrificing victims at the Great Temple in the centre of Tenochtitlan.

8. What is an Inca quipu?

a) A knotted message or record.

b) A kind of string bag carried by Inca men to store the leaves of the coco plant and a lucky charm.

c) A beaded necklace worn by nobles during important festivals in the Golden Courtyard in the capital city of Cuzco.

9. What should you do if there's an earthquake during your stay in the Andes?

a) Stay indoors.

b) Stand in a doorway.

c) Make for the Golden Garden.

10. What do the Incas value more highly than 'sweat of the Sun' and 'tears of the Moon'?

a) The leaves of the coco plant.

b) Gold and silver metalwork.

c) The work of the ordinary people in the fields.

31

Index

Acknowledgements

Design assistance
Joanne Brown

Inklink Firenze illustrators
Simone Boni, Alessandro Rabatti, Lorenzo Pieri, Luigi Critone, Lucia Mattioli, Francisco Petracchi, Theo Caneschi

Picture credits
b = bottom, c = centre, l = left, r = right, t = top
p.4cl Werner Forman Archive; p.9cr Werner Forman Archive/National Museum of Anthropology, Mexico City; p.10tl Corbis; p.12cl The Bridgeman Art Library/Museum für Völkerkunde, Berlin; p.13tr The Bridgeman Art Library/Museo Nacional de Antropologia, Mexico/Giraudon; p.15tl Hutchison Library/Liba Taylor; p.17tl Werner Forman Archive/British Museum; p.19tr NHPA/Kevin Schafer; p.21br Werner Forman Archive/National Museum of Anthropology; p.26tr South American Pictures/Tony Morrison, bl Still Pictures/Edward Parker; p.29tl Still Pictures/Julio Etchart, cr Still Pictures

Every effort has been made to trace the copyright holders of the photographs. The publishers apologize for any unintentional omissions.

Souvenir quiz answers

1 = c) 2 = b) 3 = c) 4 = c) 5 = b) 6 = b) 7 = b) 8 = a) 9 = b) 10 = a)